Fruits

Apple

Apricot

Avocado

Banana

Black Currant

Blackberry

Blueberry

Cantaloupe

Cherry

Clementine

Coconut

Cranberry

Dates

Fig

Grape

Grapefruit

Guava

Jackfruit

Kiwi

Lemon

Lime

Mango

Olives

Orange

Papaya

Passion Fruit

Peach

Pear

Pineapple

Plum

Pomegranate

Raspberry

Strawberry

Tangerine

Watermelon

www.ingramcontent.com/pod-product-compliance
Lightning Source LLC
Chambersburg PA
CBHW041521070526
44585CB00002B/37